# Battle Report

# Battle Report

SELECTED POEMS

BY

# Harvey Shapiro

*Wesleyan University Press*

MIDDLETOWN, CONNECTICUT

9/1966
am. Lit. Cont

Library of Congress Catalog Card Number: 66-23924
Manufactured in the United States of America
First edition

To EDNA

# Contents

NEWS OF THE WORLD

The past, like so many bad poems,
Waits to be reordered,
And the future needs reordering too.
Rain dampens the brick,
And the house sends up its smell
Of smoke and lives—
My own funk the major part.
Angling for direction,
I think of the favored in Homer,
Who in a dream, a council meeting,
At the bottom of despair,
Heard the voice of a god or goddess,
Though it was, say, only Polites
Speaking. Turning to a friend,
I ask again
For news of the world.

MONDAY

Everybody thinks the past is real.
The window and the skull
Admit light. The past comes through
Like that—undifferentiated,
Hallucinatory, of no weight.
Sleepless that night, he saw the
Room close-woven, a nest
Of chairs, tables, rug
The past was filtering through.
It had no odor, no
Emotion. You could not
Say that in the silences
The past came in
Like water over sand.
There was no movement.
You could not draw the blind.

And the Collectors make the rounds
Continually. What a perpetual payment
Of old fingernails, hair, skin parings:
The detritus of life, not to be grudged.
But what else they take from me
Minute by minute—heart's ease,
Zeal of success . . . .
Should I be judged,
Can I demand payment for this life
That they take from me continually?

## THE COLLECTORS

I can sit here, in the quietness,
With nothing but the refrigerator hum
To spell mortality, and imagine
The Collectors come for the sagging brain,
Lugged flesh, tired lungs.
"Right here, men!" I shout,
In that manner I lacked
All my life.

## SUNDAY MORNING

You begin to tell a story.
I perceive it is to be
Another of those unpunctuated excursions
Into the country of my failures.
You, pointing to the familiar landmarks
I, nodding in assent.
We settle back.

Concerning that time, it is written:
The secret of joy fell into enemy hands.

The widow was worked over in the upstairs
Hall last night. I could hear
The sloughing and the soft lap lap.

In the garden the daffodils turn east,
Disorderly, raunchy,
A sexual crown.

In that time, joy was a concern.
He had a void and she had a void.
They compared voids.

I asked her about anger, though my theme
Was joy. I could not tell
Which came first.

I believe we came together
Out of ignorance not love,
Both being shy and hunted in the city.
In the hot summer touching each other,
Amazed at how love could come
Like a waterfall, with frightening force
And bruising sleep. Waking at noon,
Touching each other for direction,
Out of ignorance not love.

How many times
Can you go back to the same spot
With love? I never hope to know.
We work patiently at our quarrels,
Starting them now like love,
Deliberately but with elaborate
Ease. When they catch
We marvel at the blaze,
Crowding in close.
"Inexhaustible!" we shout at one another,
Happy for the moment.
I never hope to know
How many times.

THE INJUNCTION

He went about freeing imaginary birds,
Making gestures like freeing them;
The birds were imaginary
But the gestures were real
Spirit is real even when it rides
And hides in sick motions of the body,
Where I spy it daily
And repeat to myself
The injunction:
Choose life.

THREE DAYS

On Wednesday he chose life
And went about getting breakfast
With a light heart. He looked at people,
Considered plants and stones,
Wrote letters to distant friends.
At nightfall he was back in the slough,
Hip-deep, and the stuff
Pulling him under. So he asked himself,
How is it life obviously
Does not choose you?
And what does your choice come to then?
Thursday he had no answer
And the sick spirit withered.
Friday he dropped the metaphor.

When he writes about his life
He just rakes it back
And forth. It's still
His life, so he rakes it.

FORCES

He was given over to forces that made him idle.
They came about him, rubbing their fur.
Rank with it, they stayed against his trembling,
His dizziness, his crying out
For an end to the shifting and blurring,
To the wanderings
That will not yet reveal themselves.

FOR JOB AT FORTY

Who would have thought you'd get this far,
Fingering the spots where the boils will be,
Your prosperity before you?
What a picture of absent plagues,
Dunghills, encrusted sores.
What a mark for the spoiler,
Who is there, at the corner,
And now you turn his way.

## WHAT THE WITCH SAID

I would not want to see
Gods ascending out of the earth
Or the dead living.
How can they talk so easily
Of a stone rolled
From the cave's mouth,
Of spirits crowding a ditch to drink?
What banquet
Draws them to the dead,
What tender eating?

Where the wash of the world
Filled me with the brine of
Dead things, gone things.
To wake to the illusion
Of meaning, more than
The illusion of beauty,
I have come back to
The lion and lioness,
Facing each other,
The two sides of the cloth,
To read the service again.
In my breath, the halted,
The stunned, the shattered without
Movement. Lion and lioness
Do what they will.

The night was moving to another decision
I would hear about later
And not recognize. "I am
The bitter name," said Death.
"Surely, you believe in me."

To taste in the lees of sleep.

THESE LIVES

When everything is prepared for the feast—
August high-vaulted,
The clouds a classic scroll—
The painter must have a hypo.
What's the meaning of his crying jag?
The wife calls the doctor.

The dolphin floats gently to shore
On the winds of his own corruption.
Even the gulls respect that stench.

What happens to these lives?

1. Some black Italian singing about death.
   Voices crying *Morte* in a madrigal.
   I stand like that, or
   Flow out sentimentally
   Along the edge of the city,
   Toward the narrows
   And the lighted ships.

   The riches of content,
   Weeping, weeping.

2. "You been a long time
   Coming." I come to you now
   When I can hardly.
   Beaten and then the sight
   Of skin under your blouse
   Makes me jump.
   It's what I want
   Now, and I've begun
   To pay.

I cast out
Beyond the demonic element
And the fear of death
(And the fear of death)
Into that bright water
Beyond this water
Where leviathan swims.
Communication is instant
When it comes—close
As my hand, the words on my tongue,
Though the crying in my ear
Is my own death crying.

EPITAPH

To make nothing out of nothing
Was all my study.
I had a wife to help me.
Though I came out bloody,
I made nothing out of nothing.

While someone sings "La Paloma"
The dream happens.
I walk from the couch
To my desk, the secret
In my head, the beginning
And end of my life.
I am stunned by my luck—
To have heard "La Paloma"
On the dream jukebox
In a Mexican town
While something spills into my glass
And I'm rescued from art
Once again.

A WRITER

That one wrote out of a life lived,
So I envied him. Naturally,
I could imitate his manner.
But the life lived (which, believe me,
I do not want to hear about)
Was his. To others I leave
The memory of themselves.

"Old solitary whiff-beard,"
As another poet has sung you,
I pass you twice a day
Corner of Fulton and Cranberry—
Palms up, pushing the spirit—
On my way toward work or wife,
To the subway or returning.
And you were after?
"A passage to India,"
Mottoes the bronze plaque
On the brick of the Spanish eatery
Where your leaves were first collected.
Though I remember
"Come lovely and soothing death"
Where I wound it into my skull—
A depressed kid of twelve—
As tight as the mockingbird's shuttle,
I never take up your book.
Serenely arriving, arriving,
You coast to each young poet.
Your day, delicate death,
And Century!

FOR DAVID

> Someone is writing
> "Illuminator of the Paths,"
> Or has already
> Written it, though
> I cannot find it
> On my shelf,
> Or is even now
> Walking his room
> With the book
> In his head.

Teach me the only beginning.
Point me to the god
Of the hidden time.
When I say the old names
Of mountains and rivers,
Put the map in my hand.

ADVISE ME

Since you are never sure
Whether or not the mountain
Is moving toward you,
I can understand your unease.
Breathe deeply. Pick up
The baby. Let the mountain
Move if it must. Not
Everything is in your hands.

So the angel of death whistles Mozart
( As we knew he would )
Bicycling amid the smoke of Auschwitz,
The Jews of Auschwitz,
In the great museum of Western Art.

Memory, my own prince of disaster,
My ancient of night.
In the scored silence
I see the dead.
They file past the fixed camera—
The ritual wave, and the smile,
And goodnight. For an instant
They are there, caught
In their clothes and their gestures;
Their white faces glow
In the murk of the film,
Absurdly alive. How little I own
This family of the dead,
Who are now part of night.
Memory, my own prince of disaster,
When you go,
Where's the night?

Strength cannot be resurrected
Unless it has slept in secrecy.
In the husks of forgetting
The power of memory grows.
On the day of destruction
Power lies at the bottom.
They sit on the ground.
They visit graves.

## DUMB ADAM

I forget. Was it to be
Letters of black fire on white fire
Or letters of white fire on black fire?
But here are the words.
The vines of heart-shaped leaves
Bind the trees
Yet the topmost branches remain free
To receive signals.

The freedom to glide, to coast.
The car rolling without gas,
The gull shifting from
Current to current with stationary
Wings. The clouds swing west
For another easy victory.
It is a sickness that hollows
Your life and your words.

Dumb Adam, slow-footed,
You are like the farmers
I pass in their fields;
Your world has vanished.
It is all the wind and water
Of before creation.

Along the night routes,
In the brightness of cities,
I read letters of black fire
On white fire.

The day like blank paper
Being pulled from my typewriter.
With the six
Hundred thousand letters of the Law
Surrounding me,
Not one of them in place.

DISTANCES

A world of water, out of which
The Greeks sailed,
Toward which
We set our course,
Hoping gods still
Swarm the spaces.
We have traveled such distances
Only old songs can save us.

What was ceremonially impure, he knew,
Was his life. The laws were not followed.
The god was unhonored.
Anxiety sat on every road.
To change his life, he invented
A job that promised regularity and order.
He invented love that promised joy.
In summer he sat among green trees.
The family laughed in water.
Now let the ceremony begin, he said,
In the heart of summer,
In the pure green
And the pure blue.
Let the god walk his mountain.
He can come down.

## HIDDEN

My own breath
Is hidden in the universe.
Why should I concern myself?
It rises and falls
With all the others,
So that I find it
Easy to begin.

"The Night the Old Nostalgia
Burned Down" is
The most beautiful
Title in American writing
Every night I visit it —
Crammed full of heroes,
Blonds, girls out of
My own childhood and the neighborhood.
Tenderly I light the flesh
And watch it go, like dreams:
Mother and father burning down
To the sweet music
Of Stephen Foster, hymned
In the P. S. 3 assembly.
Every day is a new beginning,
The charred remains
Softening the scent of bleak
December; background music
Against which criss-cross
Rapid images of a new life.
I leave the scene
Confident the spectacle
Has enduring worth,
Will light me a long way,
Songs to sing.

The National Cold Storage Company contains
More things than you can dream of.
Hard by the Brooklyn Bridge it stands
In a litter of freight cars,
Tugs to one side; the other, the traffic
Of the Long Island Expressway.
I myself have dropped into it in seven years
Midnight tossings, plans for escape, the shakes.
Add this to the national total—
Grant's tomb, the Civil War, Arlington,
The young President dead.
Above the warehouse and beneath the stars
The poets creep on the harp of the Bridge.
But see,
They fall into the National Cold Storage Company
One by one. The wind off the river is too cold,
Or the times too rough, or the Bridge
Is not a harp at all. Or maybe
A monstrous birth inside the warehouse
Must be fed by everything—ships, poems,
Stars, all the years of our lives.

THE DESTRUCTIVE WILL

This, then, is the child's wish:
To see the earth a dancing flood
And the new home floating free,
And all irrational, outside, inside.
The packed beasts padding through
The comforts of the living room.
And the old man, his hand forced
By the impossible command,
Compass lost and out of touch.
And all the navigational aids
Part of the swiftly moving flood.
But mainly it's the murderous beasts,
Wonderfully close and now accepted
As part of home and family:
The dumb, the fierce, the tooth and claw.
I read it in the earliest book,
Where all our childhoods signify
Themselves in open imagery.
And this is the image of the will:
To see the globe a watery blot,
History killed, pain stopped.
And this must win us to the dark,
And close our eyes, and rock our sleep,
And pray the coffin be an ark.

## THE PROPHET ANNOUNCES

*on an illustration from*
*an eighteenth-century Haggadah*

And so they arrive for all the world to see,
Elijah with the shofar to his mouth,
His hand upon the guide reins of the King,
Who rides an ass. They look so sad.
In all, a quiet scene, unless the shofar's sound
I barely hear was louder in that century.
Behind them is a tree, and on its branch
A startled bird, to say there's hope of life.
Old images of immortality.
But where's new Adam come to greet the King?
Unless this be the moment of their setting out,
And no one's heard that death's been done and even
Now the first light's traveling from the east.

# THE TALKER

*from a Midrash*

While all the choiring angels cried:
Creation's crown is set awry!
God fabled man before he was,
And boasting of His enterprise
Bade angels say the simple names
That mark in place each bird and beast.

But they were dumb, as He foretold—
When man stepped from the shuddering dust
And lightly tossed the syllables,
And said his own name, quick as dirt.
Then angels crept into their spheres,
And dirt, and bird, and beast were his.

THE MARRIAGE

When they were canopied, and had the wine
To lace their spirits in the trembling cup,
And all the holy words sang round their heads
In tribute to the maker and the vine,
He saw the leeching sea lap, like darkness,
Up her summer's gown, as if dark time
And he should race to claim the maidenhead.
When he smashed the cup, then ruin spread.
The dazzled floor showed sea and blood.
Beyond this harvest that the ritual bore
( Their mothers weeping on the farther shore)
They saw the journeying years extend.
And Zion's hill rose for their reckoning.

Violent in its blood, the dark book
Hangs like a tree of night upon the sky.
It batters history, that genesis,
Word that whelped a world up,
While priest and king and all
Raged at the syntax they were swaddled by.

And this is law, or so is said
Within the darkening synagogue
By old men, honored in their beards
By the unsealed, heroic sounds.
Celebration without end, the dark book
Whispers to the wind,
Wind cradles the destructive globe.

Outside, the night is far away.
Space is empty. One might touch,
If the necessary power were given,
All with human eloquence.
What hangs upon the tree is man.
With his blood the book is written.

EXODUS

When they escaped
They carried a pack of bones
In a mummy-coffin like an ark.
Of course they had the pillar
Of clouds by day and fire by night,
But those were like dreams
Or something painted on the sky.
God was in the bones
Because he had said,
God will remember you
If you take me hence.
This was before the miracle
By the sea or the thundering mountain,
Before the time of thrones
And cherubim. They were
Only now drawn forth
To eat the history feast
And begin the journey.
Why then should they carry history
Like an ark, and the remembering
Already begun?

On the High Priest's tunic
Golden pomegranates, silver bells.
Alexander, off for Egypt,
Was stilled by the luster of robes
Bright as that boy god's city
When it stood
Second town to Rome,
The Priest's robe must have gathered
Such light as Pharos throws.
On the day of festival
They sailed to the Island—
Jews and many others—
"Reverencing the place in which
The light of interpretation
First shone forth."
A god was translated
By those rabbis.
The sibylline oracles
Spoke Messianic prophecies.
The gates of allegory
Are never closed.

ALEPH

Oxhead, working in
The intelligence. First sign,
Alphabet's wedge.
Followed by house, fish,
Man praying, palm of hand,
Water, serpent,
Eye, and so forth—cross.
Whence to
Hebrew-Phoenician abstract
And so to Greek.
But to return to first
Signs when the world's
Complex—
The head of an ox
Blunt, blundering,
Withal intelligencer
Pushing forward, horns raised,
Stirring the matter
To make a beginning
For Amos, Homer,
And all who came first
In that sign.

These are the eminent journeyers:
Father, and son, and serving men,
The saddled ass and the gathered wood.
Across the morning, like polished stone,
Hangs the three-day-distant hill.

In the dark thicket, on the mount,
Innocence, the tangled ram,
Waits for the metaphor to kill.
It is earliest time. Light
Travels the knife, as it did the will.

Urbanity obscures the mystery.
From the fiery limits of His crown
The brawling letters broke,
In the beginning.
Violence on the historical track.
Then distances—prophet, king—
And the voltage that enabled them
To strike their meaning
And to stand. When the palmed word
Issued anodyne. The rest is mockery.

Let me borrow her corpse a little.
Over that clown in finest linen,
Over that white-dressed dummy, pretty girl,
(Dressed for a party! the daughters cried)
Let me speak a line.

The dead lie in a ditch of fear,
In an earth wound, in an old mouth
That has sucked them there.
My grandmother drank tea, and wailed
As if the Wailing Wall kissed her head
Beside the kitchen window;
While the flaking, green-boxed radio
Retailed in Yiddish song
And heartache all day long.
Or laughter found her,
The sly, sexual humor of the grave.

Yet after her years of dragging leg,
Of yellowed sight,
She still found pain enough
To polish off the final hours with a shriek.
To what sweet kingdom do the old Jews go?
Now mourned by her radio and bed,
She wishes me health and children,
Who am her inheritor.

I sing her a song of praise.
She meddled with my childhood
Like a witch, and I can meet her
Curse for curse in that slum heaven where we go
When this American dream is spent—
To give her a crust of bread, a little love.

The seven-branched candelabra glowed,
The flames like vapor ascending.
I stood in the synagogue, idle, watching,
When a man—I never saw him clearly—
Approached, and with deliberation
Began to snuff the candles, one by one.
I broke into action, seized his arm
But couldn't stop him.
Then a voice outside me cried:
The place is already defiled. Take your wife and go!
That was the end of the dream.

I never have religious dreams
But there I was,
In a prophetic setting.
The Greeks and Romans, I remembered,
Had their visionary warnings
Mainly from their mothers.
Achilles, for example, or Aeneas
When sleepwalking he had seen
Troy burning and the king's own son
Caked in his blood on the palace floor.

We came to this house by the water's edge.
The bay flashes gold in the afternoon sun
And the vapor ascends—
Says Christopher Smart—in praise of the Lord.
It's hard to begin again in truth
(I take the dream to mean I was in error).
There are still the bookcases to be built,
Pictures to be arranged upon the walls.
But yesterday I saw

Seven gulls pass overhead.
It may be tonight I will dream myself
Into a promise of life.

The past sends images to beach
Upon our present consciousness.
The sons of light war with the sons
Of darkness still. The congregations
Of the sleek and sure rule at will.

Jerome and Origen can tell
How Greek redactions of the text
Stalled at the Tetragrammaton.
And violent in archaic script
The Name burned upon parchment—

Whence springs the ram to mind again
From whose sinews David took
Ten strings to fan upon his harp.
So that the sacrifice was song,
Though ash lay on the altar stone.

## ADORATION OF THE MOON

*for Max Weber*

Sappho's moist lotus and the scudding moon
Speak to each other in a dilation upon Acheron.
Lean out of the abyss of origin four ragged Jews,
Masters of wrath and judgment, gentled by the moon.
Their tall hats rise, their faces lengthen
As o the spell is on them. Three grip
The word for ballast, while the fourth,
Beard upended, sniffs the moon-fleck as it falls.
Support them in flight, goddess,
That when the darkness comes, thy light put out,
Their candle's flame send up in steep aroma
The scholar's must.

How everything gets tamed.
The pronominal outcry, as if uttered in ecstasy,
Is turned to syntax. We are
Only a step from discursive prose
When the voice speaks from the thornbush.
Mountain, fire, and thornbush.
Supplied only with these, even that aniconic Jew
Could spell mystery. But there must be
Narrative. The people must get to the mountain.
Doors must open and close.
How to savor the savagery of Egyptians,
Who betrayed the names of their gods
To demons, and tore the hair
From their godheads
As lotus blossoms are pulled out of the pool.

As seventh sign, the antique heavens show
A pair of scales. And Jews, no less antique,
Hear the ram-rod summons beat their heels,
Until they stand together in mock show
As if they meant to recognize a king.

For they are come again to this good turning:
That from the mountain where their leader goes,
In ten days' time they greet the Law descending.
And these are ancient stories from a book
That circulates, and for them has no ending.

All stand as witness to the great event.
Ezra, their scribe, before the water gate
Takes up the book, and the people rise.
And those who weep upon the word are bid
To hold their peace because the day is holy.

Feast of the ram's horn. Let the player rise.
And may the sound of that bent instrument,
In the seventh month, before the seventh gate,
Speak for all the living and the dead,
And tell creation it is memorized.

Soul, the wanderer, fetch it out
And make it sing in holiness
And hop in God's hand all the day
And preen itself in loveliness.
Five afflictions are the way.

Because the soul is living wick
And flames in its vitality,
Deny yourself both food and drink.
Imitate mortality.
Soul will shake itself and flee.

Because the soul is unity,
Within the coupling dark lie still.
Let body in its agony
Cry to have itself fulfilled.
Soul will know itself unwilled.

The soul is spirit, and spirit shines
As pennies do in a cupped hand.
But the hand, if washed, can shine so too.
Keep precious water from your skin
And spirit will not stay within.

The soul is an unchanging thing.
It cannot weight itself with grit.
But body, when anointed,
Puts on a like purity.
Slime yourself, and soul will flee.

Soul, like wind, is lifted up,
Like waves, and like the sea spray.

Let a man go barefoot, and he must
In his heaviness draw dust.
And soul, unhoused, is on its way.

Soul, the wanderer, fetch it out
And make it sing in holiness
And hop in God's hand all the day
And preen itself in loveliness.
Five afflictions are the way.

"The word moves a bit of air,
And this the next, until it reaches
The man who receives the word of his friend
And receives his soul therein
And is therein awakened"
Rabbi Nachman's preachment on the word,
Which I gloomily thumb
Wondering how it is with me
That I am not yet on the first
Rung (and many with me!).
To move a bit of air!

If a man ask, can he have
This thing, whether it be
An infusion of soul, or souls,
Steadfast to complete the journeying?
Words moving a bit of air
So that the whole morning moves.

SUMMER

The glazed day crumbles to its fall
Upon the tiny rout of fishing
Boats. Gulls convoy it down,
Lengthening their cries that soon
Will rake the evening air; while some,
Silhouetted on a strand
In a jumbled line of target ducks,
Watch as ebb tide drains the bay.

From a rotted log upon
The shore, like the other beached
Mutations, shell and weed, I wait
For Highland Light to cast its eye.

July unhives its heaven in
A swarm of stars above my head.
And at my feet, flat to the water
That it rides, the lighthouse beam,
A broken spar, breaks its pulse.

"What have I learned of word or line?"
Ticks on, ticks off; ticks on, ticks off.
The bay, that was a clotted eye,
Is turned to water by the dark.
Only my summer breaks upon
The sea, the gulls, the narrow land.

In the midst of words your wordless image
Marches through the precincts of my night
And all the structures of my language lie undone:
The bright cathedrals clatter, and the moon-
Topped spires break their stalk.
Sprawled before that raid, I watch the towns
Go under. And in the waiting dark, I loose
Like marbles spinning from a child
The crazed and hooded creatures of the heart.

The struck animal, blurred
By subsequent hours, lies
Upon the road, hunched fur and spirit.
At night, drawn by the hum of power,
Then doubled into pain, sight smashed,
It caught the radicals of
Descending speed, their brilliance.

Or the boy in Dreiser's novel,
That blind head, felled
By the big city hotel,
Its monolithic shine and scramble.
Even Crane, who tried to make
A shining steel structure of a bridge
Lead him out, caught by the brilliance
That kills, in America.

As at the movies close,
Man alone, against the wall,
Watches the lights move in,
The fugitive hatless there.
And we, thrilled into our fear,
See the enormously wheeled clatter,
Glistening, never in error,
Rise to break his back.

The snow of another winter
In slow, granulating fall
Ticks the world to an electric stop.
I stand and stare
Where the lighted town
Stops swinging in the drift—
This lighted town where couples race
All spilt with laughter
As the year with thorn.

And brighter than promise sings
The reddening tree,
O brighter than hope!

Time drifts upon the banished child.
But in this, his season, he steps forth,
And in us all.
Caught on a windy corner
Of my thirtieth year,
I am what I was,
Sure of the kingly prize,
The monstrous child,
Wishing the world to be
Filled with the dazzling snow.

While brighter than promise sings
The reddening tree,
O brighter than hope!

Being a tourist, what I did was right:
To set the native Indian in his lair,
There where three crosses bind the sky
And mark the holy ground. Mary's Day,
And from surrounding hills they came
With banners, drink, and wooden pipe
Into the church all richly dressed.

Because we traffic with the centuries
And take our meaning where we can,
Upon the mud-packed floor I knelt me down.
Pine needles green as carpet to the holy feet
That danced before the images; brown
Saints dazzled by the candle shine.

And where the altar stood, beneath
The green cross wooden as the sky,
The crowded iconography that drifted there:
A bearded king, the genius of the place,
A faceless woman grieving for her son,
The familiar son upon his cross of bones.

But where he rode, I saw his smothered form
Wrapped and tied, until the features gone,
The bloodless son looked down on all his world
From the very womb that mothered him.
Here was a conception to be gathered in.

Yet, touristing, I do their meaning wrong.
There was no womb, no mother, and no son
But Deity, violent in his imagery,
Annihilating history to break the form.
I saw him in that first night from which,
With cataclysm, they shall bring him forth.

*Section IV*

BATTLE REPORT

1.

I praise an age that has no monuments,
That if millions die within a war—
A few I knew, a few I saw go down—
They die forever, and what's to be said?

2.

It is always a prayer to the remembering Muses:
Remember me. Remember through all time
That I sing this,
You who write the genealogies
And the spirits crowd round without number.

3.

The Adriatic was no sailor's sea.
We raced above that water for our lives
Hoping the green curve of Italy
Would take us in. Rank, meaningless fire

That had no other object but our life
Raged in the stunned engine. I acquired
From the scene that flickered like a silent film
New perspective on the days of man.

Now the aviators, primed for flight,
Gave to the blue expanse can after can
Of calibers, armored clothes, all
The rich paraphernalia of our war.

*[73]*

Death in a hungry instant took us in.
He touched me where my lifeblood danced
And said, the cold water is an ample grin
For all your twenty years.

Monotone and flawless, the blue sky
Shows to my watching face this afternoon
The chilled signal of our victory.
Again the lost plane drums home.

### 4.

No violence rode in the glistening chamber.
For the gunner the world was unhinged.
Abstract as a drinker and single
He hunched to his task, the dumb show
Of surgical fighters, while flak, impersonal,
Beat at the floor that he stood on.

The diamond in his eye was fear;
It barely flickered.
From target to target he rode.
The images froze, the flak hardly mattered.
Europe rolled to its murderous knees
Under the sex of guns and of cannon.

In an absence of pain he continued,
The oxygen misting his veins like summer.
The bomber's long sleep and the cry of the gunner,
Who knows that the unseen mime in his blood
Will startle to terror,
Years later, when love matters.

5.

My pilot dreamed of death before he died.
That stumbling Texas boy
Grew cold before the end, and told
The bombardier, who told us all.
We worried while we slept.
And when he died, on that dark morning
Over Italy in clouds,
We clapped him into dirt.
We counted it for enmity
That he had fraternized with death.
From hand to hand
We passed in wonderment
The quicksilver of our lives.


6.

In the blue oxygen, what I saw,
My valve fluttering its song,
My ears tight to the static.
I perceived that I was rocked
In the body of the plane.
Rarefied air frosted my lashes.
Congealed breath sparkled my scarf.

So gloved and chuted, wired into my bones,
I rode the day. Austria,
An ant's plan underfoot.
In that perilous seat above cities
I mixed into my own breathings
And waited, exposed as a stone.
Sunlight through plexiglass above my head
Was light without sun, a blue wash of cold.

This I recall, seated in my room,
Having sloughed off the glory and the pose
That place where the oxygen faltered
And the mask of my face went closed,
And they pried me, sleeping, from the sea.

Walker under water, can you believe
That even now the sun touches
That phalanx of fins, the vectoring Forts?
It is mainly cold I remember, and the warmth
When my mask, clotted with breath, grew dark.

### 7.

I turn my rubber face to the blue square
Given me to trace the fighters
As they weave their frost, and see
Within this sky the traffic
Fierce and heavy for the day:
All those who stumbling home at dark
Found their names fixed
Beside a numbered Fort, and heard
At dawn the sirens rattling the night away,
And rose to that cold resurrection
And are now gathered over Italy.

In this slow dream's rehearsal,
Again I am the death-instructed kid,
Gun in its cradle, sun at my back,
Cities below me without sound.
That tensed, corrugated hose

Feeding to my face the air of substance,
I face the mirroring past.
We swarm the skies, determined armies,
To seek the war's end, the silence stealing,
The mind grown hesitant as breath.

*Distinguished contemporary poetry in cloth and paperback editions*

ALAN ANSEN: *Disorderly Houses* (1961)

JOHN ASHBERY: *The Tennis Court Oath* (1962)

ROBERT BAGG: *Madonna of the Cello* (1961)

ROBERT BLY: *Silence in the Snowy Fields* (1962)

TURNER CASSITY: *Watchboy, What of the Night?* (1966)

TRAM COMBS: *st. thomas. poems.* (1965)

DONALD DAVIE: *Events and Wisdoms* (1965); *New and Selected Poems* (1961)

JAMES DICKEY: *Buckdancer's Choice* (1965) [National Book Award in Poetry, 1966]; *Drowning With Others* (1962); *Helmets* (1964)

DAVID FERRY: *On the Way to the Island* (1960)

ROBERT FRANCIS: *The Orb Weaver* (1960)

JOHN HAINES: *Winter News* (1966)

RICHARD HOWARD: *Quantities* (1962)

BARBARA HOWES: *Light and Dark* (1959)

DAVID IGNATOW: *Figures of the Human* (1964); *Say Pardon* (1961)

DONALD JUSTICE: *The Summer Anniversaries* (1960) [A Lamont Poetry Selection]

CHESTER KALLMAN: *Absent and Present* (1963)

VASSAR MILLER: *My Bones Being Wiser* (1963); *Wage War on Silence* (1960)

W. R. MOSES: *Identities* (1965)

DONALD PETERSEN: *The Spectral Boy* (1964)

HYAM PLUTZIK: *Apples from Shinar* (1959)

VERN RUTSALA: *The Window* (1964)

HARVEY SHAPIRO: *Battle Report* (1966)

JON SILKIN: *Poems New and Selected* (1966)

LOUIS SIMPSON: *At the End of the Open Road* (1963) [Pulitzer Prize in Poetry, 1964]; *A Dream of Governors* (1959)

JAMES WRIGHT: *The Branch Will Not Break* (1963); *Saint Judas* (1959)